Shall we now remember everything great and splendid that took place within these walls?..
Shall we recollect the magnificent festivities they witnessed and the remarkable events which occasioned them? Shall we give the names of those who visited this palace, who hastened from all ends of the earth to visit this palace which suddenly shone forth in the remote and previously gloomy North?
Oh! The future historian of the Winter Palace will have to present us many unusual and interesting things, valuable for us and beautiful in the extreme! The history of the palace is the history of Russia itself...

Anatoly Bashutsky

THE IMPERIAL PALACES
THE WINTER PALACE

The Winter Palace was built in 1754—62 to the design of Francesco Bartolomeo Rastrelli. The huge dimensions of the palace and the architect's idea to erect the building "for Russia's glory" could be explained by its purpose — he designed the main residence of the Russian Emperors. The palace was built during the reign of Peter's daughter Elizabeth, but its first residents were to be Peter III and Catherine the Great. Before 1917 all the Russian monarchs had their apartments in the palace, and its state rooms were used for official ceremonies, formal receptions and balls. The façades of the palace, although repeatedly reconstructed, have changed little (except for the colouring of the walls and the sculptures on the parapet which were replaced in the late 19th century). The reconstruction work was led by the eminent architects — Yury Velten, Jean-Baptiste Vallin de la Mothe, Antonio Rinaldi, Giacomo Quarenghi, Ivan Starov, Carlo Rossi and Auguste Montferrand. A dramatic event in the history of the palace took place between 17 and 19 December 1837 when a conflagration completely destroyed its interior decor. Nevertheless, Vasily Stasov and Andrei Briullov reconstructed the interiors by March 1839, within an amazingly short period of 15 months. Another immense amount of work was carried out by the architect Alexander Sivkov in the 1920s—1950s when the palace was converted into a museum.

THE MAIN STAIRCASE

The Main Staircase, "indeed, unrivalled in Europe as regards the beauty of its position and extension", was created by Rastrelli, and Stasov preserved its magnificent design during his restoration of the building after the fire. The design of the staircase is based on the contrasts of light and shade and of various spatial elements. From the first, shady flight of stairs the viewer

suddenly finds himself in a spacious interior struck by its abundance of light and magnificence of decor. Its space seems to spread out in mirror reflections and the infinity of the illusionary painting on the vault. Stasov made some alterations in the decor: he reproduced the former Baroque motifs in moulded ornaments, but decorated the columns with grey Serdobolye granite instead of previously used artificial marble and replaced the carved wooden balustrade with a marble one. He also adorned the ceiling with a painting representing gods on Olympus, a work by the 18th-century Italian Diziano Gasparo which had decorated another room in Rastrelli's interiors. This composition, together with the sculptural allegories of *Fidelity, Justice, Grandeur, Wisdom, Equity* and *Abundance* set in niches, emphasized the significance of the main Imperial residence as a dwelling of earthly gods and an abode of virtues. The staircase played an important role in the layout of the palace — two enfilades of state rooms, the Neva and the Main Suites, diverged from it. In the 18th century the staircase was named the Ambassador Staircase — it was used by ambassadors presenting their credentials, while in the 19th century it was known under another name, the Jordan Staircase, which came from annual religious processions starting from it to the Jordan Pavilion erected on the ice of the Neva during the Jordan Festival of the Blessing of the Waters.

THE GREAT HALL
OF FIELDMARSHALS

The Hall of Fieldmarshals is the first room in the Main Suite leading to the Hall of St George (Great Throne Room) and the Great Church. It was built according to the design of Montferrand in 1833—34 and became notoriously famous because it was in this interior that the disastrous fire of 17 December 1837 broke out. Montferrand left empty the space between the wooden wall of the Hall of Fieldmarshals and the adjoining Hall of Peter the Great for the outlets of the heating shafts of the palace pharmacy and its laboratory which were located on the ground and basement floors. Several sparkles were enough to set the wooden partitions on fire. Once the flames burst out there, it was already impossible to stop the conflagration. This majestic hall was conceived as one in a group of interiors commemorating major events and notable figures of Russian history — it was used to display portraits of the most famous Russian fieldmarshals: Count Piotr Rumiantsev-Zadunaisky, Prince Grigory Potiomkin-Tavrichesky, Count Alexander Suvorov-Rymniksky, Prince Mikhail Kutuzov-Smolensky; Count Ivan Dibich-Zabalkansky and Count Ivan Paskevich-Erivansky. The portraits of the celebrated soldiers were saved during the fire and returned to the Hall of Fieldmarshals in 1839, after Stasov's reconstruction of the interior to "its former appearance". In the middle of the 19th century two large battle paintings, works by Horace Vernet and Gottfried Willewalde, and the sculptural portrait of Count Paskevich were added to the military-historical "display" of the hall. During World War I, at the decision of the Imperial family, the Hall of Fieldmarshals was used, like other large rooms in the palace, as a military hospital.

THE HALL OF PETER THE GREAT
(THE SMALL THRONE ROOM)

This hall created by Montferrand in 1833 was reconstructed to the design of Stasov with minor alterations. The main architectural and conceptual emphasis in this interior dedicated to the memory of Peter the Great is a composition centred around Jacopo Amigoni's allegorical canvas *Peter the Great and Minerva*, painted after the death of the Emperor, in a semicircular recess. The portrait was trimmed with jasper columns and topped by a pediment bearing the Imperial crown. An honourable place under Peter the Great's portrait was occupied by a historical relic — the throne of Empress Anna Ioannovna made in London by the English master craftsman Nicholas Clausen in 1731. The wooden base of the throne was mounted in a massive frame of gilded silver and its back was embroidered with the state emblem of Russia. Numerously repeated elements of Imperial attributes — Peter the Great's monograms, crowns and double-headed eagles — play a prominent role in the decorative scheme of this interior. Even the embroidery in dark crimson velvet serves as a background for a number of compositions including the state emblem of Imperial Russia upholstered in silver (the upholstery was replaced not only because it wore out, but also due to changes in the design of the emblem). It was owing to these symbols as well as to the companion paintings in the lunettes featuring famous battle scenes of the Northern War — the Poltava Battle and the Battle of Lesnaya — that contemporaries regarded this interior as "a palladium of Russian grandeur and glory", which both perpetuated the memory of Peter the Great and glorified the might of the Empire created by this outstanding Russian autocrat.

THE ARMORIAL HALL

The White Gallery, which had come into being in the late 18th century, received a new meaning in 1830 when sculptural groups of Russian warriors in chain-mail and helmets executed from models by Vasily Demuth-Malinovsky and Nikolai Tokarev and provided with the emblems of the Russian provinces fixed on spear shafts were installed there. The sculptural compositions included banners and lances decorated with double-headed eagles and laurel wreaths. When reconstructing the hall after the fire of 1837, Stasov extended it and made some alterations in its design, but the figures of the soldiers were restored by the sculptor Julius Streichenberg to their former look, since their patriotic emphasis determined the role attached to this hall in the Great Suite of the Winter Palace. Previously known as the White Hall, the interior was then named the Armorial Hall — even the chandeliers were decorated with representations of the emblems of the Russian provinces. The lavish use of gold emphasized the distinctive character of this interior illustrating the state structure of Imperial Russia: "the beautiful gilding totally covered lengwise the fluted columns" which were spaced along the perimeter of the hall; the choir balustrade was gilded; and gold was also used to paint trophies in imitation of stuccowork.

THE 1812 WAR GALLERY

The 1812 War Gallery is the most famous among the memorial interiors of the Winter Palace. The inauguration of the gallery designed by Carlo Rossi was held on 25 December 1826, the anniversary of Napoleon's expulsion from Russia, in the presence of generals, officers and soldiers awarded for their participation in the War of 1812 and in the Russian Army's campaign abroad in 1813—14. The gallery housed the banners of all Russian military units which took part in this war. Hanging on the walls lined with red cloth are 332 portraits of those who were generals during the war or received the rank immediately after it. Blank areas were left to commemorate the 13 dead heroes whose likenesses could not be found. All the portraits were produced in the studio of the English painter George Dawe who was specially invited to Russia for this purpose. The gallery houses also the representations of the leaders of anti-Napoleonic coalition and the commanders-in-chief of the allied armies — Friedrich Wilhelm III, the King of Prussia, and Franz Joseph I, the Emperor of Austria. During the fire of 1837 all the portraits were rescued and hung in the gallery again after Stasov had completed its reconstruction. Dawe's portrait of Alexander I was later replaced with a more imposing likeness of the Emperor painted by Franz Krüger.

THE HALL OF ST GEORGE
(THE GREAT THRONE ROOM)

The Hall of St George was created by Stasov to replace the destroyed interior which had been decorated to the designs of Quarenghi in the 1790s. Stasov considerably altered the decor preserving only the general proportions and architectural features of the interior — Quarenghi's polychrome marble facing of the walls and columns and his painted ceiling were not restored. Stasov made the decoration more austere: he used white Carrara marble brought from Italy and designed a suspended metal ceiling with deep caissons adorned with incised and gilded copper ornaments. "The marble clothes" of the Great Throne Room were made by the Italians Ignazio Rossi and Paolo Catozzi led by the architect Nikolai Yefimov. The Italian master craftsman Francesco del Nero created a marble low-relief of St George slaying the dragon which shielded as it were the throne place under it (dismantled in 1940). Notable decorative elements in this important interior were the state symbols of Russia — double-headed eagles were used even in the decor of the chandeliers. Consecrated in 1841, the Hall of St George played an important role in the entire official history of the Russian ruling family. It was in this hall that the State Duma was inaugurated in the early 20th century.

THE GREAT CHURCH

The Great Church was created during Rastrelli's construction of the palace and consecrated in 1762 as the Church of the Resurrection. In 1763, when the icon of the Saviour was brought there, the church was consecrated once again, this time to *The Vernicle* icon. Stasov, who reconstructed the interior after the fire of 1837, was set the task that the church "shall regain its original aspect" — it was thought particularly important to keep the church unchanged as a place which had seen major events in the history of the ruling family (baptisms, marriages and taking oaths). The architect decided not only to reproduce the Baroque style, but even to go back to Rastrelli's original design as drastic alterations had been made there a long time before the fire — the dome had been covered and the ceiling made flat. Stasov reopened the dome as the main feature of the Orthodox church's design and symbolism. His only important alteration was the dismantling of Rastrelli's huge stoves decorated with tiles because they became unnecessary — after the fire the palace was provided with air heating (large stoves were built in the basement floor to supply hot air to all the rooms). The removal of the stoves allowed the architect to provide the church with three entrances instead of the single one which had existed before. A significant part of the decor — the figures of angels over the columns, the heads of cherubs

decorating the ceiling and ornamental motifs, and the sculptural groups of the iconostasis — were made of papier-mâché. The idea to use this material first came to Stasov in 1820 when he restored the palace church in Tsarskoye Selo. The concept was realized in the Winter Palace by the sculptors Denio Adt, Vasily Demuth-Malinovsky, Piotr Svintsov and Julius Streichenberg. The superbly carved iconostasis surmounted by the Crucifixion with the interceding St John the Baptist and the Virgin, the altarpiece mount and the pulpit (all dismantled in 1940) were made by the carver P. Cretan. The icons produced by the Russian icon-painters Ivan Belsky and Ivan Veshniakov and by the Italian Francesco Fontebasso were saved during the fire and set in the same way as before. Fontebasso's monumental works — the Evangelists in the pendentives and the composition of *The Resurrection* on the flat ceiling of the entrance room — perished during the fire and were reproduced by Fiodor Bruni (the Evangelists) and Piotr Basin (the ceiling painting). The church (a cathedral since 1807), was the final chord in the symphony of visual and conceptual imagery into which plunged the participants of the so-called entrées of the Imperial family — the carefully regimented formal processions from private apartments (the Malachite Room) through the halls of the Neva and Main Suites to the Great Throne Room or to the Great Church.

THE MALACHITE ROOM

The Malachite Room was decorated by Alexander Briullov during the reconstruction of the palace after the fire. This interior, the main reception room in the private apartments of Nicholas I's wife, Alexandra Fiodorovna, was designed by Montferrand in 1830. Briullov partly retained his design, but used malachite instead of jasper. The columns, pilasters and fireplaces were made at the Peterhof Lapidary Works in the technique of "Russian mosaics" — by pasting thin plaques of malachite, a semiprecious green stone, so as to build up a single pattern. The blend of these elements with the abundant gilding of the vault ornaments, doors and capitals sent contemporaries into raptures as they did not know "what to marvel at" in this "temple of wealth and taste"— "the luxury of materials or the luxury of the artist's thought" . The southern wall faced with white artificial marble was decorated, as before the fire, by Antonio Vighi's pained allegorical figures symbolizing *Day*, *Poetry* and *Night* which were executed on canvas and pasted to the wall. The interior bordering between the state halls and private apartments of the Empresses served as a reception room until the revolution. During the "most august entrées" the Cavalry Regiment Guard lined up near the Malachite Room. It was considered an important privilege "to stand behind the cavalier guards".

THE WHITE (SMALL) DINING ROOM

This interior is known as a room where the bour-geois Provisional Government was arrested during the night from 25 to 26 October in 1917. It is probably owing to this fact that the Dining Room has become the only interior surviving intact in the Winter Palace, except for the Gothic Library (most of the last Russian Emperor's interiors have been destroyed in the 1920s when the palace was redesigned to serve as exhibition rooms of a state museum). The White Dining Room was decorated to the plans of the architect Alexander Krasovsky in 1894—95 for the marriage of Nicholas II, then the heir-apparent, to Alice, the Princess of Hessen-Darmstadt (Alexandra Fiodorovna). Krasovsky redecorated the Dining Room replacing the Pompeian style employed by Briullov in 1839 by the new, Rococo style, with its extravagant use of moulded ornamental motifs including sea-shells, garlands and scrolls. The rocaille motifs were used in the pattern of the parquet floor. The furniture produced from the drawings of the architect Nikolai Nabokov, also imitated this decora-tive style. The subtle stylization was enhanced by some authentic 18th-century works — tapestries manufac-tured at the St Petersburg Tapestry Factory (three allegories of the continents — *Asia, Africa* and *America*) and a crystal chandelier of English work.

THE ROTUNDA

The concept of this interior was suggested by the composition of round Classical temples with a skylight coming through the vault. Reconstructing the Rotunda created by Montferrand in the 1830s, Briullov largely altered both its design and decor: he designed its cupola in the shape of a hemisphere and faced it, as a fire prevention measure, with earthenware pots. Contemporaries regarded the new spatial and technical solution of the hall as a true achievement — they admired the "lofty, daring and slender stone cupola replacing the partly flat wooden ceiling". Briullov's metal gallery supported by brackets divided the interior into two tiers, making it more commensurate with man's figure. Situated next to the private apartments of the Empress, the Rotunda was used for formal ceremonies, concerts and festivals. Thus, during the reign of Nicholas I, on Christmas Eve, Alexandra Fiodorovna usually organized parties, with richly decorated Christmas trees and presents, for her own children and those from the narrow circle of the court families. It was the Empress Alexandra Fiodorovna who introduced the custom of decorating fir-trees on Christmas in Russia. From the mid-19th century a representative character of the Rotunda was emphasized by the display of portraits of the Imperial family members there.

THE STUDY-BEDCHAMBER
OF ALEXANDER II

Throughout the 19th century the Study-Bedchamber was regarded as a memorial interior. The room was decorated by Giacomo Quarenghi for Alexander I at his birth. Later Grand Duke Konstantin Pavlovich, the future Emperor Nicholas I and his son Alexander Nikolayevich spent, consecutively, their childhood years there. The decor of this remarkable room in which three monarchs grew up, had no alterations during repairs. The exquisite majesty of Classicism dominated this interior during the 19th century. After the fire of 1837 Briullov reproduced Quarenghi's design "down to the last detail". Thus, unlike other rooms decorated in a new fashion, he left intact a typical example of Quarenghi's style there — the decoration of the flat ceiling with pictures set in geometrical frames along its perimeter which was echoed by the austere pattern of the floor. The walls were divided into panels; the columns of the alcove and the panels were of artificial marble. The low-relief decorations over the doors and on the wall of the alcove were fashioned by the sculptor Francesco Denio in keeping with the Classicist tradition. As any bedroom, the interior had an alcove separated with columns and "designed so as to instal a bed there". However, as Nicholas I recalled, the children did not sleep in the alcove, "because it was

thought to be overheated from the two stoves in the corners". On becoming the Emperor, Alexander II used this interior as his private room in which he could work and have a rest, hence its name. After the October Revolution of 1917 the Study-Bedchamber was one of "historical rooms", a part of the display the Museum of the Revolution had in the Winter Palace.

THE GOTHIC LIBRARY

The Gothic Library was created for Nicholas II to the designs of Alexander Krasovsky in 1894—95. The Gothic was then regarded as the most suitable style for the decoration of this kind of interiors. The decor of the room not only evoked in the viewer tangible associations with mediaeval monastic libraries but even gave to him or her a general impression of plunging deep into the past. The Gothic ornamental motifs (lancet arches, trefoils and four-leaf rosettes) were also used in the design of the two-tiered bookcases, the main item of furniture in the room, and employed in the carved patterns of the banisters and the gallery of the upper tier. The unoccupied portions of the walls, between the lower tier of the bookcases and the gallery, were covered with red leather stamped in gold. A prominent feature of the interior was an immense fireplace built of Bremen sandstone "in the Gothic style" by the marbler Grazioso Botta. The decor of the fireplace included alternating heraldic figures — "the Romanov gryphon and the Hessen lion", i.e. the family coat of arms of the Romanov dynasty and that of the Hessen-Darmstadt house, from which Empress Alexandra Fiodorovna descended. The Gothic Library, together with the Study, the Billiards Room and the Reception Room adjacent to it, made up the working section of the Last Emperor's apartments.

THE WHITE HALL

The White Hall was created by Briullov during the reconstruction of the palace after the fire. This two-lighted room, characterized as "huge" or "colossal" by contemporaries, was decorated in 1841 for the wedding of the heir-apparent, the future Emperor Alexander II, with Maximiliana-Wilhelmina, the Princess of Hessen-Darmstadt (Maria Alexandrovna), as the main hall of his apartments. The decoration of this room included the moulded representations of trophies, allegorical and mythological figures and scenes — four sculptural female figures symbolizing the Arts; low-relief depictions of Juno and Jupiter, Diana and Apollo, Ceres and Mercury, Vesta and Neptune; a frieze with putti; and elaborate ornamental motifs. The excess of moulded and sculptural decor was "neutralized" by well-thought-out proportions and an impressive colour scheme of the interior based on white. The bright accents of the mahogany gilded doors, the ormolu chandeliers, the dark marble fireplace and the red upholstery of the furniture served to enliven the monochrome decor of the White Hall. During Alexander II's reign the hall had a special use — festive receptions were then held not in the northern part of the palace as during the reign of Nicholas I, but in its southern section, adjoining the private apartments of the Emperor and the Empress.

THE GOLDEN RECEPTION ROOM

The Golden Reception Room was the main state room in the apartments of Alexander II's wife, Maria Alexandrovna, decorated by Briullov for her marriage to the heir-apparent in 1841. It was not by chance, therefore, that the design of this room, according to the architect's concept, echoed the decor of the main reception room of Alexandra Fiodorovna — the Malachite Room. Originally the walls and vault in the Golden Reception Room were faced with white artificial marble and only thin moulded ornaments on them were emphasized by gilding, whereas the furniture was "totally gilded". The colour scheme was enhanced by the bright blue of the panels painted in imitation of lapis lazuli. The contrast was brought out by the blue tone of the curtains over the doors and walls and the upholstery of the furniture. A distinctive place in the decor of the hall was given to the white marble fireplace which formed a single composition with a mosaic picture, a mirror trimmed with jasper columns, and a moulded low-relief. In the 1860s—1870s the artistic design of the interior was markedly changed: the walls were covered with gilding from top to bottom, probably to the design of Vladimir Schreiber. In the reign of Alexander II family gatherings were often held in this room and Christmas parties took place there.

THE CRIMSON STUDY

The Crimson Study was decorated by Briullov in 1841 and functioned as a state study of Maria Alexandrovna and her dining room. In 1858, Stackenschneider altered the design of this room (the vaults were removed and the ceiling made flat) and redecorated it. He replaced the upholstery but left its crimson colour scheme unchanged.

THE BOUDOIR

The decor of this room, Maria Alexandrovna's boudoir and private study, was originally created by Briullov, but in 1853 Harald Bosse completely rebuilt it. He designed for Maria Alexandrovna a refined interior stylized in the Rococo spirit — with delicately outlined carved and gilded motifs, a virtuoso use of mirrors creating an illusion of space and inset paintings. A particularly intimate character was given to the Boudoir by the design of an alcove divided from the main interior by a step, a low bronze railing and a drapery. At first, the architect wanted to highlight that recess by decorating the alcove walls with white fabric, whereas the rest of the room was lined with crimson one, but eventually he preferred a uniform colour scheme. The pomegranate-coloured textile for panels on the walls, the furniture upholsteries, the draperies on the windows and doors and the decoration of the arch of the alcove were commissioned at the Cortier Factory in France. To decorate the overdoor panels, Harald Bosse used paintings from the Hermitage reserves. For "a convenient placement of the furniture" the fireplace was shifted from the longer wall to that pierced with windows. Behind the alcove, Bosse created a staircase leading to the room of the Imperial couple's children situated on the ground floor.

THE ROOMS OF BATTLE PAINTINGS

The suite of five state rooms looking onto Palace Square was decorated by Briullov in a similar way: the ceilings were lavishly decorated with painting in imitation of stuccowork and with gilding and the walls were painted in turquoise. The uniform character of the decorative solution was unusual both for the palace interiors restored after the fire of 1837 and for the work of Briullov, an architect whose "wealth of invention" and "variety of fantasy" amazed his contemporaries. It was due to the fact that the rooms were intended to serve as a single picture gallery made up of five sections. After 1839, the suite was used to house battle paintings illustrating the main events in Russian war history of the 18th and 19th centuries — the Northern War, the Swiss and Italian campaigns of Alexander Suvorov and the Russo-Turkish wars — hence the name of the suite (its interiors differed only by their ordinal numbers: the First Room, the Second Room, etc.). The rich painted decor of the ceilings in imitation of stuccowork, the design of the door frames as portals, the elaborate patterns of the parquet floors, all adds to the representative, imposing appearance of the suite. For their majestic atmosphere the rooms ranked with the best state apartments of the age of Classicism. During the reign of Alexander II, the Rooms of Battle Paintings were often used for official ceremonies.

THE ALEXANDER HALL

Briullov's project to design a memorial hall in honour of Alexander I in place of the Cavalier Guards' Hall and the passage rooms created in 1834 was carried out during the restoration of the palace after the fire. The architect found a brilliant spatial and structural solution of the huge double-lighted hall. Its original ceiling — with fan vaults and low load-bearing cupolas — became the main architectural and artistic emphasis. The impression of majesty and space led contemporaries to describe the hall as an interior "in a Byzantine taste". The architect used elements of another, Gothic style in the details of its decor too — the clusters of thin columns and fan vaults emphasized the upward thrust of the architectural masses. The decor of the interior made it a memorial not only to Emperor Alexander I (his formal portrait painted by George Dawe was set against the background of the crimson velvet embroidered with laurel wreaths, and above it was a low-relief with the profile representation of Alexander "in the guise of a Slavic deity, Rodomysl" symbolizing wisdom and bravery), but to the War of 1812 and the 1813—14 European campaign of the Russian Army as well. The frieze was decorated with enlarged copies of Fiodor Tolstoy's medals telling in allegorical form about these historic campaigns and with the allegorical figures of Glory. The decoration of the mouldings was mainly

based on military motifs. The white marble fireplaces
served as pedestals for large moulded compositions of
arms and armor. The four huge battle paintings also
emphasized the memorial character of the hall. When
during a wedding in the Imperial family it was neces-
sary to observe, after the main, Orthodox procedure,
some other religious rite, such ceremony was usually
held in the Alexander Hall.

THE NEVA SUITE

The suite of rooms running along the northern façade of the palace and looking onto the Neva was designed by Rastrelli with a special purpose — it led from the Main Staircase to the Throne Room. The Neva suite consisted of five rooms: the four antechambers and the Fore Hall directly adjoining the Throne Room. In the 1790s, after the creation of the new Throne Room (Hall of St George), the suite has lost its initial function and was redesigned by Quarenghi. The architect created three new interiors instead of the five former rooms: the Concert Hall (in place of the Fore Hall), the Large Fore Hall (equal to the three antechambers in size), and the Fore Hall leading to the Main Staircase (in place of the First Antechamber). The sumptuous Baroque decor gave way to the refined austerity of Classicism. Restoring the Neva Suite after the fire of 1837, Stasov retained its layout but made the decor of the room more restrained and monumental: the subtle interplay of beautiful colour combinations of the artificial marble facing the walls and columns gave way to a predominantly white colour scheme; small decorative elements disappeared and the forms grew larger. "Although seemingly nothing has changed, everything has been remade there," contemporaries commented understanding that "the recreating and restoring artist, though drawing on the laws of the previous version, cannot fail to leave an

imprint of present-day art on his work and the mark of his own talent."

The Concert Hall

Owes its name to large concerts and theatrical performances which took place there. The function of the interior was reflected in its decor — the statues of Classical muses and deities made by the sculptor Joseph Hermann were set at the second tier. They perfectly matched the allegorical figures with the attributes of the Arts painted in imitation of stuccowork which were placed at the top of the walls and in the lunettes.

The Large Fore Hall

The largest of the state rooms in the palace, had another name, the Nicholas Hall, from 1856, as the Emperor's portrait painted by Franz Krüger was hung in the centre of the longer wall there. The air of majesty characteristic of this hall was imparted to it by the three-quarter columns of the Corinthian order spaced along its perimeter and the austere painting of the flat ceiling with imitations of caissons.

The Fore Hall or the Small Fore Hall

Which was aptly called "a lobby, but a lobby worthy of the Imperial house" by a contemporary, was decorated in a more complex colour range than the two other halls of the suite: its walls were faced with yellow artificial marble which perfectly blended with gilding. After the fire the ceiling was embellished with Giacomo Guarano's

painting The Sacrifice of Iphigenia which had adorned the Concert Hall until 1830. During large balls the Neva Suite, illuminated by thousands of candles and highlighted by colourful military uniforms and exquisite dresses, was a fantastically beautiful and spectacular display.

P-2 PUBLISHERS

specializes in publications on art, such as art books,
picture postcards, posters and calendars.
The present edition continues the series of miniature
art books *Many-Faceted St Petersburg*
to be published in Russian and foreign languages:

Imperial Saint Petersburg;
Orthodox Saint Petersburg;
The Imperial Palaces: The Hermitage;
The Eternal Festival: Peterhof;
Tsarskoye Selo: Palaces and Parks;
Treasures of the Russian Museum;
The Peter and Paul Fortress

———

Concept of *Many-Faceted St Petersburg* series
by Leonid Pozdeyev and Sergei Vesnin
Selection and text by Tatyana Pashkova
Designed by Nikolai Kutovoi
Photographs by Pavel Demidov, Victor Savik
and Oleg Trubsky
Edited by Maria Lyzhenkova
Translated from the Russian by Valery Fateyev
Managing editor Nina Grishina
This publication has been produced with the assistance
of the St Petersburg City Division
of the Federal Postal Service

Licence 062197 of 3 February 1993
ISBN 5-900-530-08-6
Printed and bound by Ivan Fiodorov Printing Company,
St Petersburg (№ 3626)